The Baby
Massage Book

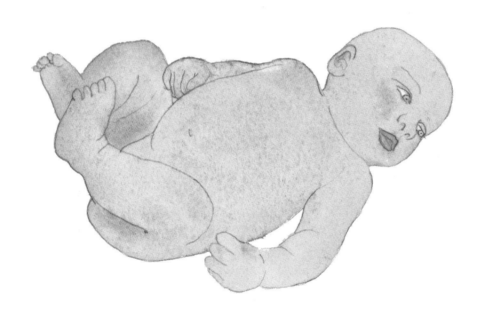

The Baby Massage Book

Shared growth through the hands

by
Tina Heinl

Water-colour illustrations

by
Julie Depledge

Coventure, Ltd. London, Boston

Originally published by Coventure Ltd., London, 1982

Coventure, Ltd. London, Boston
25 New Chardon Street #8748
Boston, Massachusetts 02114

Library of Congress Cataloging in Publication Data

    Heinl, Tina.
    The baby massage book: shared growth through the hands/
    by Tina Heinl; water-colour illustrations by Julie Depledge.
    p. cm.
    Includes bibliographical references (p. 62).
    1. Infants—Care. 2. Massage for infants. 3. Parent and child.
    I. Title.
    RJ61 .H3824 1990
    649′ .5—dc20   90-193   ISBN: 0-904575-15-2
    CIP

Set in Rockwell typeface

Printed in Korea

To those who have helped me develop,
in particular
Peter, Sophia and Matheus

Contents

Acknowledgements

I should like to thank the many friends who played a part in bringing this book to life. In particular to Ian Fenton for his encouragement, to Annette Dolphin, for her invaluable help in editing the book, to Antonio Roberto Teixeira, for taking the photographs for the massage section, to Patricia and Hannah Keenan who kindly agreed to be the models for the photographs, to Julie Depledge for the fruitful discussions and the beautiful drawings, to the parents who have written to me with their impressions of the massage, and to Didi Macedo for giving me the text on the premature baby stroking. I should also like to thank Evaline Xavier without whose help I should not have had the time to write the book, and finally especial thanks to Peter for his support.

My thanks to all those who provided the photographs:
A.R. Teixeira, S. Bauer, J. Henshaw, J. Depledge, B. Brown, A. Mariani, F. Coubert, P. Sawaya, I. Fenton, P. Heinl, S Everett, Vision International.

Preface

This book was born from my experience of massaging my two children during the first months of their lives, and later from teaching this baby massage to other parents with young children. These experiences opened my eyes to the importance of touch from the very beginning of a human being's life. They made me realize that touch plays a major role in the process of bonding and, therefore, the development of trust, between the parents and their children. In addition having practised the massage for some time, I felt a conscious expansion of my sense of touch. In particular, I discovered the importance of my hands, because of their ability to touch and their sensitivity to receive the sensation of being touched. This gave me so much pleasure and confidence in handling my children, and also I saw immediate and yet long-lasting benefits stemming from the massage for all of us, that I accepted the challenge to share my experiences, observations and ideas with a wider public.

Since the inception of this book, I have had the vision in my mind of a story-teller in India sitting under an enormous old fig tree, surrounded by his audience, telling stories from his life, slowly and with great feeling. Each person listening to the story-teller distils a meaning from his tales which is personally important for them in leading their own lives. It is in the same spirit that I should like this book to be seen and used.

In the first chapter I describe how I came to use the baby massage with my two children, and all the benefits we derived from it. I also tell how I started to teach the massage to other parents. While trying to understand the implications of this massage in my life, I attempted to visualise the role of the sense of touch during all the stages of development of a child from conception to birth. In the second chapter I explain my views that from the very beginning of the formation of a baby in the mother's womb, the essential emotional bond between the mother and her child starts to develop. This attachment arises out of the intense and constant body contact between the mother and her unborn child. This bonding can also be shared by the father as by touching his partner, especially her pregnant belly, he comes closer to his unborn child.

In the next section I expand the ideas which have developed while I have been practising the massage, on how important touching can be as a means of communication between children and parents. It helps to maintain the mental and physical health of all involved. The book then continues with an account of how parents in other cultures use massage and body contact in the handling and care of their children.

The baby massage technique which I have used, adapted from a traditional Indian massage, is described in Chapter 5. Each movement in the sequence is illustrated in full. The introductory section explains a few practical points to make the massage easy for anyone to learn, to enjoy, and to incorporate into their daily lives. Although in the interests of clarity I have chosen to use throughout the book the feminine pronoun for the parent and the masculine for the unborn child and the baby, I should like to stress that no discrimination is intended, especially since I believe that fathers could benefit enormously from massaging their children.

In the next chapter I describe the physical and emotional

effects of the massage on babies and parents. These benefits have been observed both by myself and by other parents who have practised the massage. They include a better and more regular sleeping pattern, a stronger sense of security for the baby, a more confident handling of the baby by the parents, better feeding and digesting and a strong spacial awareness acquired by the baby. All these advantages lead to a more balanced development of the baby as a person. The last chapter deals with the method I have developed for teaching the baby massage.

Two appendices are included at the end. The first gives a list of natural oils that can be used for massage. For each oil I give its source and some of its properties. The second appendix is a suggested list of books for further reading on the several themes touched on in this book.

1

My Personal Experience with Baby Massage

Soon after the birth of my first child, Sophia, I received a present which was to have a great effect on my life. The present was Frederick Leboyer's book "Loving Hands", which describes a traditional Indian art of massage of children. When I started reading the book, I was immediately fascinated. I felt that it opened a new way for me to relate to my child. The day was a beautiful, sunny Sunday in early Spring, and I decided to massage my daughter. The three of us, my husband, Sophia and myself, spent a very pleasant afternoon, completely absorbed in learning the massage and taking photographs of it. That day marked the beginning of a very deep, simple and beautiful experience.

From then on I massaged Sophia, and one and a half years later my son Matheus, nearly every day until they were ten months old. When they grew older and started crawling and trying their first steps I began to massage them less frequently, until I stopped when they were two years old. Although my husband did not massage the children, he often observed the massage, and bathed the children afterwards. I believe that this experience with the massage made all of us more aware of our own bodies, and especially of our sense of touch. My husband and I became more relaxed and confident in handling, in the literal sense of the word, our children.

I have often been asked what made me continue the massage with such persistence. Looking back at those early days I am still able to relive the pleasure I found in this daily routine, when I could be together with the children in such a relaxed atmosphere. Massaging meant enjoying ourselves. There were, nonetheless, some days when I was very exhausted, especially if I had slept badly, when I nearly decided not to bother with the massage. But it was on those days that I realised how calming it was for me to sit on the floor and enjoy the feeling of my hands touching the little body in front of me. Soon this alone would cause my worries and tiredness to slip away.

It was during this time that I began to be very aware of my hands, and started to obtain great satisfaction out of touching as well as being touched. It was almost as if I were rediscovering my sense of touch, and the variety of sensations to which my hands were capable of responding. It seems to me that by doing the massage I also gained a better understanding of my children as persons in their own right, with their own bodies and identities, different from myself. At the same time the massage led to a very deep attachment between us. The daily massage was especially rewarding with Sophia who had had a difficult birth and who had developed jaundice, because of which she had to spend her first three days under ultra-violet light in the incubator of a special baby unit. As a result, the close contact between us was ruptured for this period after her birth, and the daily massage seemed to heal the distance between us, and to allow a strong bond to be re-established.

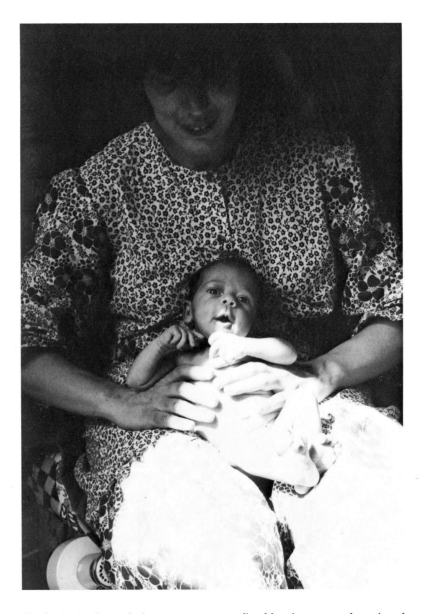

At the beginning techniques are not too refined but it seems to be enjoyed anyway.

Soon I realised that my small daughter began to cry not only when she was hungry, and I observed that offering her the breast was not always the answer to her problems. She also needed very much the comfort of our presence, and to be held close to our bodies. By touching her body with our hands we were talking to her in the way she could understand. Somehow we were showing our love to her by 'feeding' her skin. As the days went by she became a very active baby, eager to grasp her surroundings, and to understand them through her hands, mouth and eyes. Yet she remained quite contented and calm.

Months later when Sophia began to walk and talk, and became more and more independent, I was still surprised to see how much touching her had a calming effect on both of us. So often to bring Sophia to my lap and to hold her close to me was, and still is, the one way that we can relax ourselves enough to be able to sort out our differences.

The birth of my second child Matheus was a very moving experience during which I was able to understand the beauty of giving birth in a natural way. The previous experiences of the birth and daily massage of my daughter made me particularly aware of my own body during my second labour. I felt that I could open myself more easily and work through each contraction, finally pushing him with my own strength into the outside world. Massaging Matheus then became a very natural habit, a part of my daily routine from which Sophia did not feel excluded. While I was massaging Matheus, Sophia used to play in the same room and also derived benefit from this peaceful time. Sometimes she like to help me perform the massage, and this gave me the opportunity to show her how to touch her brother. At other times she would just play busily with her toys in the corner of the room. Through watching the massage she learned very soon to play gently with her brother, and to examine his body without hurting him. I frequently had to admire how careful she was when she touched the baby. Soon they became friends despite their differences and jealousies.

For me the half-hour spent in this active but relaxing interaction with Matheus was an ideal way to balance the attention that I wanted to give to both my children. Every parent with more than one child knows how difficult it is to be attentive to the simultaneous demands of several young children, and to divide one's time fairly between them. I found that when I massaged the children we were able not only to relax, but also to satisfy our need to be touched, in other words to feel that we were loved. Through the massage we learned that there are times to be together and times to be alone without fear of not being loved. The massage helped us to trust each other, and allowed the children to develop more easily the necessary attachment to us, their parents, after which they could feel safe to explore their surroundings.

When my son was five months old, my husband made a short film of one of the massage sessions. I was interested to know how clearly it showed the techniques of the massage, and how much one could grasp of the complete ritual by simply watching the film. We showed the film to friends, and were delighted with their enthusiasm. From that time on I started to teach other parents this simple art of how to massage their own children. The experience of talking to parents and other interested people about baby massage stimulated my ideas about the role of touch in our lives, both in general and in particular during the first months together with one's new baby. The idea of teaching the massage to small groups of parents with their babies proved to be a very good means, not only for learning the massage technique, but also to give us the opportunity of sharing our experiences concerning pregnancy, birth and the first months with the baby. Often the groups were able to provide support and understanding for common problems occurring within family life.

These experiences made me aware of the importance of this early body contact between the newborn baby and his parents. By massaging their children, parents seem to become more aware of their hands as part of their bodies, more able to perceive another person. They become more sensitive and open to the

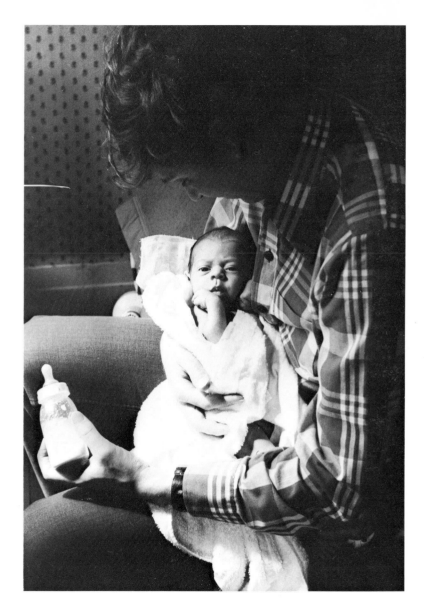

Sharing massage sessions makes the father much more involved with the new-born baby.

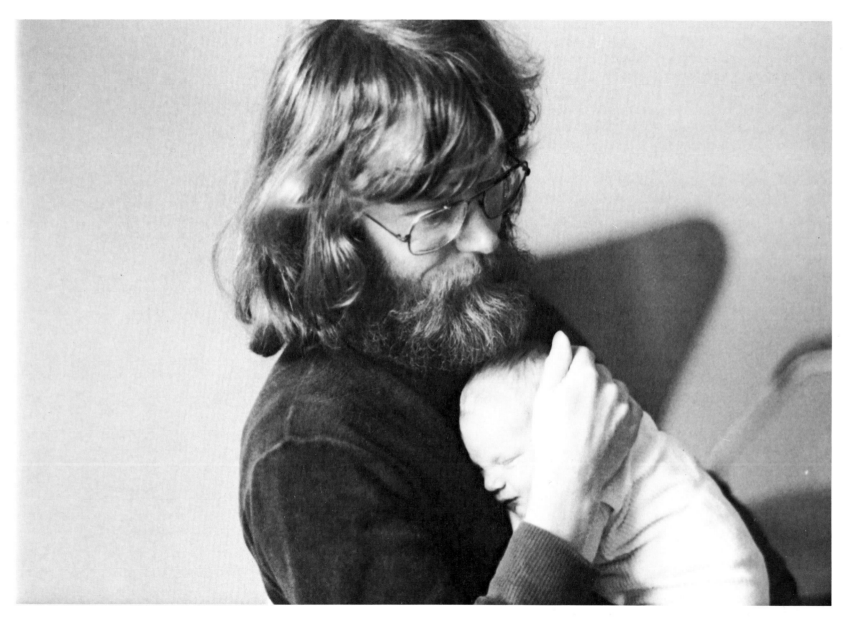

Holding can produce great peace for the parent as well as the baby.

4

impressions which arise through this contact. Parents learn not only to know their child, his body and all his characteristic reactions and expressions, but they also become aware of their own particular way of touching their child, of pacifying him and of holding him so that he feels safe and secure.

Siblings may have a more dynamic relationship when both have had strong physical bonding with their parents, such as that brought about by massaging.

2

The role of touch throughout our lives

From the very beginning, life is based on an intimate and deep contact between cells, that adhere to each other and exchange information. The creation of a new life occurs when the sperm of the father enters the egg cell of the mother and they fuse. At this moment a substance is produced around the membrane of the fertilised egg, making it impossible for other sperms to enter it. After the fusion, whose importance is that it brings together the genetic material of both parents into a single nucleus, the fertilised cell starts to divide, first into two, then into four smaller cells. So this divisional process is continued for some time, forming a mass of cells covered by a sticky membrane. During this period the embryo migrates from its original position in the Fallopian tube near the ovary, to the womb, where the uterine wall has become prepared for its reception. The embryo attaches itself to the wall, and becomes embedded deep within it. In this safe place it will develop rapidly in the next nine months into a baby that is ready to be born. Thus the development of the embryo-child takes place entirely within the restricted surroundings of the womb of the mother. This provides a secure and stable environment with a constant contact between the mother and the baby. The womb expands to accommodate the baby's growth, and the fluid in the amniotic sac provides a cushioning protection for the developing foetus.

The skin is one of the first organs to be formed during the development of the embryo-child. It has many functions, and it is primarily in the skin that the sense of touch resides. From the earliest stages of the embryo-child, and throughout life, a dynamic communication takes place through the skin, between the individual and its outside environment. The skin might be said to form a bridge between the internal and the external worlds of the human being. The foetus lives in an aquatic environment in the womb, being surrounded by the amniotic fluid. The skin is prepared gradually for life in the atmosphere outside the womb, and from the sixth month of pregnancy it is covered by a creamy white substance, the vernix, that nourishes, protects and lubricates the skin until after birth. During labour this substance helps the baby to slide more easily down the birth canal, and reduces friction. It seems that the vernix is also able to protect the skin of the new-born baby during the first days of its life, and that is the reason why usually, the baby is not given a bath or washed immediately after birth. In contact with the air this creamy substance dries out and flakes off by itself.

Very early during the course of its development, even in the first month, when the umbilical cord is long enough, the foetus begins to move in the womb. By stretching his limbs and his back, and by kicking and turning somersaults, he comes into a more active contact with the wall of his mother's womb. These movements which the mother feels by the third month, are the first clear sign that she is carrying a living individual inside herself. It is very often as a result of the kicking movements that

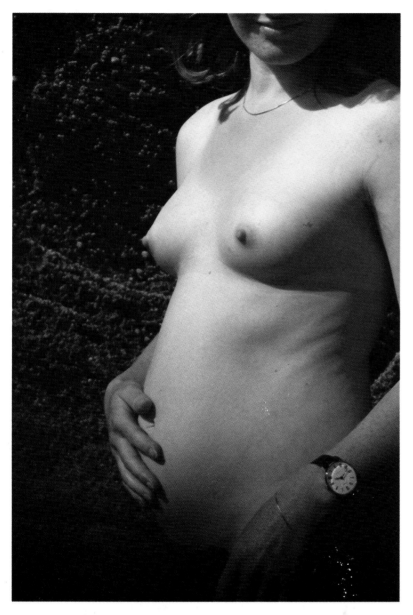

Perhaps touch is reassuring even when the baby is still in the womb.

the mother is able to relate more easily to the process that her body is going through. She is attentive to her baby's kicking, which is for her a means of communication between herself and her child, whom she begins to know through this physical contact.

From the beginning of pregnancy many mothers like to touch, stroke and massage their bellies, trying to feel and indeed to grasp the person inside themselves. It is an attempt to bring together the sensations and feelings that they are receiving from inside their bodies with those obtained through their hands, using their sense of touch. For the expectant father, touching the woman's belly that is carrying his child also brings great satisfaction, and allows him to come closer to and understand better his partner and his feelings about the baby. By using his hands he can grasp the reality of the baby and allow his feelings to develop on a sound basis. This is the beginning of the experience of fathering. Far too often in our western culture fathers have had to play the role of the outsider during pregnancy, and sometimes one has been liable to forget that they have contibuted at all to the existence of the baby.

Just before birth, the lower end of the amniotic sac that has enclosed the embryo-child during its development, breaks, and the fluid in it comes out. Usually labour starts at that point. During labour the child is moved down the birth canal. The body of the baby is pushed slowly forward by the strong waves of contraction in the walls of the womb and the birth canal. In a rhythmic way, the mother works to bring the baby into the outside world.

While the baby is gradually being pushed through the birth canal, the skin of the baby is rubbed by the pressure of the walls. In particular, the scalp, face, eyes, nose and mouth are strongly stimulated. This friction may be seen as a stimulating massage, preparing the baby to adapt to his new environment. Once outside, he takes his first breath, and as his lungs fill with air, his life outside the womb has begun.

The long duration of labour in humans compared to nearly all other mammals seems to emphasise the importance of

7

Feeding is not just supplying milk; eye contact and holding is vitally important.

8

stimulation of the skin by the friction that occurs during the passage of the baby through the birth canal. It might be compared to the instinctive licking practised by all other mammals except humans, which occurs immediately after the birth of their offspring. It is well known that this licking by the mother is essential for the survival of the youngsters, and that they will perish if the licking is not performed. By licking her offspring, especially the head, eyes, nose and anal region, the mother stimulates their breathing and other bodily functions, which are essential if the offspring are to adapt themselves rapidly to their life outside the womb.

The human baby is born in an immature and dependent state, unable to look after himself. His appearance and expressions are directed towards attracting and keeping the attention of his mother. The new-born baby perceives his new surroundings and the presence of his care-giver using, in particular, his sense of touch which resides in his skin. He feels the proximity of his mother. She, for her part, also needs the presence of her child. Her body is stimulated by his presence and by his suckling of her breast.

It is important that, from the very beginning, close body contact be established between mother and child, in order that the essential bonding between them be able to develop. It would appear that almost all mothers, even when they have gone through a difficult time during the birth of their child, experience a deep need to touch their baby as soon as he is born. It is not enough to be told that one has given birth to a healthy boy or girl, or even to see the child. The longing for actual bodily contact is very strong for both mother and child. How can one calm the anxiety, the fears and the curiosity of a mother, except by letting her hold her own child close to her, so that, through all her senses, she can slowly absorb this new person in her life? The function of all the helpers present at the birth should, be to allow the desires of the mother to be satisfied, and to help her gain the confidence to establish a strong bond with her child.

It seems that if a mother has been allowed to hold her baby

In parts of Nepal the practice of massaging, using oil as a protection against the sun, is an essential part of motherhood.

9

In the touching there emerges a new caring dimension of masculinity.

immediately after the birth, she is then able more easily to give her partner the opportunity to participate in the first moments of their baby's life in the outside world. Like the mother, the father also has a strong need to hold his child, so that he can bridge the gap between his expectations and the reality of his new-born baby. Fathers who have been present during the birth of their child, and who have had the opportunity of participating actively in it seem to be able to feel much closer to their child. By their very nature, fathers must play a passive, supporting role during pregnancy. Is that the reason why one tends to consider the father an intruder during labour, when his partner is at her most vulnerable and has the greatest need of his support? He, more than any other person, has the trust of his partner, and his physical presence, holding her hand, massaging her, and even receiving the baby as it is born and giving it to her, can only be a great advantage for the family life that these three participants have now started.

Touching any object gives it a greater reality, and we all have an intrinsic need to touch someone to whom we feel close. Holding a baby, and providing him with a secure supportive environment in her arms gives a great deal of self confidence to the parent. It forms a means of communication that both baby and parent can understand and enjoy. The experience of having a baby, and so becoming a parent, brings to light an often forgotten part of oneself. The contact with, and handling of, her baby may cause the parent to become more conscious of her own babyhood and childhood. In the dynamic process of becoming a parent one is very much influenced, perhaps subconsciously, by the way one was handled and cared for by one's own parents.

As I became more conscious of my own hands, while touching my children during the daily massage, a vivid image suddenly struck my mind. Inside my own hands I saw the image of my mother's hands, my father's hands, my grandparent's hands, and so on, back in time. What I was doing with my hands was a result of all the stimulation and comfort I had received throughout my childhood from being touched myself.

10

A Photograph taken after massage and bath. There is no doubt about the mutual enjoyment of father and baby.

3

Touching as a means of communication with our children and our partner

With the arrival of the baby in the family, and the busy time for everyone involved, the difficulties of adapting to the new life often cause parents to forget to care for each other as man and woman. Especially now in our society, where the nuclear family is usually small, and is very often living in isolation and without the support of an extended family, parents seem sometimes to suffocate in their expectations of themselves. Communication between the parents is essential during this period, in order that they can adapt to their new roles within the family. The demands of a new-born baby are very real, and they take up much of the time that the two parents used to have for each other. In the beginning, one very often feels too tired to engage in any social activities. Now should be the time to enjoy uncomplicated contact within the family. For the parent who has spent the day looking after the baby, at the same time adapting to his rhythm, and also trying to cope with the household, the joy of being taken into the arms of their partner and embraced is a real change, and a great stimulus for continuing to care for their baby. Similarly, both partners need to be reassured that they are still loved, and that their baby has not taken their lives over completely. Why not then try to share with each other what one has also been giving to the new baby!

Caring for a new-born baby is, however, not a one-way process. That is to say, it does not just involve the mother and the father looking after their child, giving up much of their time and their energy to this task. The new-born baby himself also helps the mother and father to accept and develop their parenthood. The parents need the child as much as he needs them. It is, therefore, an interaction between three people, each of whom is stimulated by the others, although since the mother has carried her baby within herself for nine months, she usually has from the beginning a greater familiarity and a closer contact with the child.

It is true that any baby could survive without his own mother provided that adequate physical care were given. However, while the baby was developing during pregnancy, the mother was also using this time to go through the various changes in her own body that have equipped her for her new role of primary care-giver. The experience of birth is as important for the baby as it is for the mother, and a good experience provides a better start for the development of the relationship between them. Immediately after birth, the mother is able not only to breast-feed her baby and thus provide the necessary nourishment for his physical growth, but she is also optimally attuned to the emotional needs of her baby. Through the close interaction between her child and herself, the mother gives her baby the opportunity to attach himself to her, and so to feel safe to explore her, and his surroundings beyond her. Through contact with his mother, the baby learns to relate not only to her but also to others.

Although fathers do not have as intense a body contact with their child as the mother, they also become 'emotionally pregnant' with their child. In this sense the need for a close contact is always there, even if these needs tend, in our society, to be repressed or not to be given enough attention. At this time it is the mother, more than anyone else, who is able to allow her partner to become the father of their child.

It seems that the first image on which the baby focuses, and which he comes to know and distinguish very well, is the human face, in particular that of his mother holding him to her breast or

We tend to forget that babies like just lying and listening on our chests.

giving him the bottle. Even as a new-born baby he is already able to use all of his senses to examine his new surroundings, although in the first weeks he is best able to perceive them through his sense of touch. Looking at the development in the infant of the different senses of touch, sight, hearing, smell and taste, it is known that the sense of touch is the most fully developed sense of the baby at birth. The other senses come into the picture progressively later. Hearing develops fully before the sense of taste, this is followed by smell, and finally the visual sense. Vision develops rapidly only after birth, as the baby acquires a depth of focus, and becomes able to see distant as well as close objects. Thus he is gradually able to apprehend a progressively larger world through his eyes. Nevertheless, the sense of touch remains of great importance to the baby throughout his development for the comprehension of objects, and the interpretation of his visual sense.

By touching the baby, the parent is stimulating the skin, in which the touch receptors are situated. Through these receptors, which are distributed not only under the skin, but also in the muscles and the joints, the impressions of touch are felt. Touching is perceived by both the parent and the child, and they react to each other in synchrony. In other words, when the child is touched and so made to feel comfortable, he will express pleasure, and the parent will be encouraged to continue. The very basic feeling of trust, that comes from being held securely and lovingly, is primarily formed through direct body contact between the baby and his parents. This contact is maximal during the first months of the baby's life. Holding the baby, and giving him this sense of security, understanding his needs by observing his expressions, provides the baby with a firm basis for his own feelings, and so teaches him to trust his care-givers. The feeling of trust, which forms the true attachment between the parents and their baby, is essential for the full physical and mental development of the baby. In those early days, eye contact between the baby and his parents also plays a very important role. By looking at each other, they learn to know each other's

13

The beginning of a family is a very delicate and sensitive process. Everyone involved is learning to cope with his new role, and more than ever, the trust of each one of the partners will be tested in continuously changing ways.

faces, down to the last detail. They learn to judge each other's expressions, and to react accordingly. In becoming aware of both his parents, using all his senses, the baby is then able to become aware of himself as a separate individual.

Communication between the baby and his parents and others at this stage, is almost entirely non-verbal. The baby is not able to understand our spoken language with all its nuances, although he is adept at picking up the feelings expressed in the tone of the voice. It is interesting to observe how we change our tone and way of speaking when talking to a baby. We use a much softer voice, and we try to come close to the baby and look at his face. Very often we touch his face or hands to attract his attention and to make sure that he is looking at us. Thus we try to assure ourselves of a non-verbal response from him.

We should not forget that the early life relationship of touch includes the child's own touch explorations.

4

Massage as used in different cultures

Massage has been practised for centuries in many cultures. It is used for several different reasons. Physiotherapists use massage for medical purposes, to activate various muscles of the body, to achieve relaxation especially in painful areas and also to stimulate the blood circulation. A good example of massage used for medical reasons in emergency is heart massage for cases of heart failure. Massage has also been known for a long time to improve the general well-being of an individual, and is also a way of giving pleasure. The positive effects of body contact through massage are well recognised. These include activation and relief of tension in different systems of the body, deep relaxation, relief of pain, a calming support in situations of stress and grief, erotic stimulation, and not least a communication between two people using the hands.

In massaging another person, one can take in that person's body as consisting of parts of the complete person, using one's hands and also the other senses. Touching is always a two-way stimulation, in which one touches the other body, or even parts of one's own body, and immediately one is aware of getting feedback from the part that has been touched. This is the reason why massage gives a heightened awareness of their bodies to both of the persons involved in the massage. It is impossible to hide one's feelings during massage, and here one must always remember that the body never lies.

In many tropical countries such as parts of India, Pakistan, some African countries and the West Indies, baby massage is part of a traditional way of handling children. Almost from the moment of birth, the babies are massaged, often initially by their grandmothers or by the 'midwife'. Very often the mothers are also massaged, at least for the first few weeks after the birth. Later, when the mother feels fit, she will usually take over and continue this daily ritual of massaging her child.

Massage helps the baby in several different ways. By rubbing him with oil, his sensitive skin is protected against the sun, he is helped to relax and to become more flexible, and his muscles are stimulated to develop and grow stronger. Not least, the massage of the face is thought to improve the beauty of the baby's profile. The natural plant oil used for the massage, which is well absorbed by the baby's skin, nourishes the skin, and prevents it from drying out. Some oils, such as mustard oil, which is traditionally used in India, has beneficial effects on the respiratory system of the baby, and is said to provide protection from colds. By using oil warmed to hand temperature, the massage gives a feeling of well-being and warmth. Very often the massage of the baby in traditional cultures is performed in the middle of the village, in the open air, under the hot sun. Thus all the impressions of his surroundings play a role in the effect of the massage on the baby. Yet the mother and her child are able to put the busy life around them into the background, and enjoy their personal interaction together.

The all-important skin contact also comes through breast-feeding. With some South-American native babies this might last until they are already starting to walk. They may also be bathed in the river and massaged until after that stage.

17

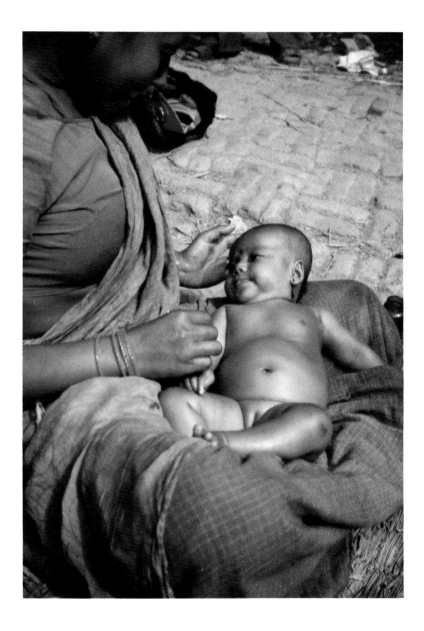

Massage in Nepal.

The practice of massaging the mother during labour, and for the first weeks after the birth, helps to relieve the tension in her body that has gone through so many new experiences. By relaxing, she is then able to let the stresses which have accumulated during pregnancy and birth slip away from her. By having her own needs understood the young mother learns, through this model, to care for her new baby.

Especially in India and neighbouring countries, the practice of massage remains an important habit throughout life. Children and adults are frequently massaged, and there is a common custom of a 'Saturday oil bath' which consists of a full body massage with a natural plant oil, and afterwards a long bath.

In many primitive cultures, the handling of babies involves a constant contact of the baby with his mother. In some tribes of South American Indians, the babies are constantly carried by their mothers during the day, until they start crawling and walking. In the first months of their lives, they spend all of their time in a skin to skin contact with their mother. During the night they sleep in the same hammock as their parents, close to their mother's breast, so that they are free to feed when they feel hungry. In such cultures, bathing in the river is a widespread habit, and because of the hot and humid weather, children tend to spend much time playing in the water, with their parents when they are very young. The effect of the water on the skin might be seen as a form of pleasurable and stimulating massage.

The approach to the caring of babies and young children in these cultures, is to keep them always close to the mother, and thus they are immediately introduced into the life of the community. They learn to know their surroundings by observation, and by experiencing them from their safe vantage point. The life of the community with its different activities and rituals, is open to the child from birth onwards. In this way he is accustomed to participating in, and finds it easy to accept his culture. The skin to skin contact, the constant carrying of the baby on his mother's hips or back, can be compared to a continuous comforting massage. By carrying their babies in this manner, the natives are recognising the dependent state of the new-born babies, and are able to provide them with a security that, at the same time, leads to a successful adaptation to their natural environment, the tropical forest. In these cultures, it is understood that a baby needs the constant stimulation of his environment in order to be able to adapt to it, and to survive in it. All these forms of contact, either massage or the constant carrying of a baby with the mother, result in a natural communication between the baby and his care-givers. It is interesting that, by carrying their babies in slings the women in these cultures have much more freedom of movement than we have when we rely on prams and push chairs. In many ways our life-style in modern societies imposes great barriers for a deep and natural contact between our children and ourselves.

Massage has been performed traditionally as a means of protecting the new-born baby against the weather in countries with hot climates. Yet it can be adapted to our lives, giving us the possibility to enjoy interacting with our children in an age-old way, which is also fun for both participants. For the parent, massage brings a break to her busy life. It provides a welcome and peaceful interlude, after a working day outside the house, or during a day of looking after a baby. In order to do the massage successfully, one has to relax oneself, to empty one's own mind, forgetting at least temporarily all worries and problems. The half-hour of massage and bath is a chance for both the parent and the baby to relax, and so to digest the impressions of the day.

Massage is also a process of learning about each other. Both the parent and the baby are engaged in exploring each other's ways of communication. Massage is like a dance in slow motion, a very harmonius activity, involving all one's senses, producing different movements that are repeated again and again, in a symmetrical and synchronised way.

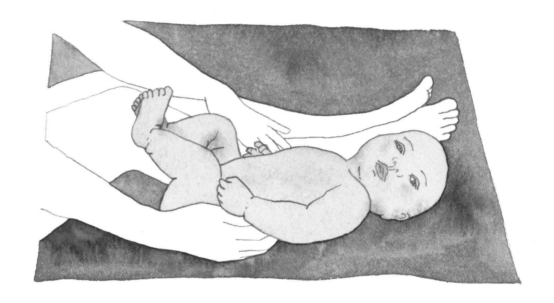

5

The Practice of Baby Massage

The massage described in this book is not simply a technique to be learned mechanically, but is a time of the day chosen by the parent to be with her baby, when they can mutually discover their bodies at their own pace and rhythm. In this chapter I shall draw attention to some practical points that may make the start of this simple ritual easier.

This baby massage can be used from the first week after birth, provided that you take care not to touch the healing navel. In the first weeks, the massage should consist mainly of rubbing the baby with oil very lightly. There is no need to perform all the movements at the start, but you will first learn to know the body of your new-born baby through your hands. When the baby is about a month old, the complete massage may be performed safely in full.

The time

The massage can be performed at any time of the day when your baby feels comfortable, not too tired or too hungry. I have always preferred to massage in the middle of the morning, half an hour after a full feed, so allowing the baby to have digested his milk, before starting the massage. The reason for choosing the morning was that I noticed how calm and contented my children were immediately after the massage, and that the calming effect lasted all day. It is important to allow enough time for the massage, on average it takes a good half-hour, from the beginning to the end including the bath. It is better not to massage at all than to try to do it too quickly. Remembering that the massage will affect both of you, it is therefore important to consider the best time of day when you will also feel able to relax, and enjoy the time together with your child.

The room

This should be warm so that your baby will feel comfortable without his clothes. It is usual to perform the massage sitting on the floor, with your baby lying on your legs, and it is useful to have enough space around you, especially when older children are playing in the same room. Sometimes soft music helps one to concentrate better on the massage. The room should be full of light, and in summer, on warm days, it is possible to do the massage outside, providing that the baby does not feel cold.

It is best to lay a towel on the floor to sit on during the massage. The oil to be used is warmed up to hand temperature by putting the bottle of oil in a bowl containing hot water for a few minutes. It is advisable to keep some tissues on hand to clear up possible accidents that the baby may have during the massage. Make sure that you are wearing comfortable clothes that allow you to bare your legs, so that the baby can have a good skin to skin contact during the whole massage. After having prepared the room, make sure that your hands are warm before picking up the baby, as an abrupt change in temperature may make him cry. I always used to undress my children on the floor on the towel that I would then sit on. From this moment on I was entering the ritual.

In the first weeks of the baby's life you may prefer to sit in a chair without arms, and so feel more comfortable to handle your small baby safely. It is important to allow your baby to see your face, giving him the opportunity to make eye contact with you. For that reason, when you first start the massage, if you are sitting on the floor with your legs together in front of you, bring your knees up slightly, so that the baby is nearer to you, and will be able to focus on your face. Babies often cry if they cannot see their parent during the first part of the massage. You may not feel comfortable to sit on the floor without any support for your back. You can start by sitting with your back to the wall. However, to feel one's body free to move, and being able to use the arms without restrictions, helps one to concentrate solely on the massage.

Feeding

The massage should never be performed immediately after a full feed. However, in the early sessions, and especially when the baby is very young, he may need a little milk during the massage. You should satisfy his needs when he indicates that he is hungry, by stopping the massage, feeding him, and then continuing afterwards where you left off.

Crying

At the beginning the massage is a novelty for both of you. It is very common for the baby to cry and he should be reassured by you in your usual way, by talking to him in a soft voice, by picking him up and bringing him close to you, and giving him a cuddle before continuing the massage.

The massage

After you have undressed your baby, lay him on his back on your outstretched legs, allowing him to find a comfortable position. Pour some oil into your hands, so that you can feel if its temperature is right. Slowly and gently, rub the oil into the baby's body, in the sequence: shoulders, arms, hands, chest, tummy, legs and feet. Now you can start the movements. Each movement should be repeated at least three times in a slow continuous motion, letting the whole surface of your hands and fingers touch the baby's body.

Let the impressions and sensations that you are receiving through your hands reach deep into your consciousness. Observe your baby, always being aware of his face and his expressions, so that you will know how much pressure you should apply when touching the baby in each movement. The baby likes to be touched firmly, so you need not be afraid of letting him feel your hands warm and secure on his body.

The baby is massaged from the centre towards the periphery of his body, for the simple reason that this movement is easier to perform, and does not drag the skin. These movements activate the blood circulation in the skin and also stimulate the circulation in the rest of the body.

The illustrations show you in detail how to perform the massage step by step. I have found it important always to perform the whole sequence, and always in the same order, starting from the chest, and massaging the front of the body before turning the baby over and massaging the back, and then coming finally to the face. However, if the baby does not take to the massage immediately, or if you do not feel confident enough, in the first few sessions, the baby should be massaged a little each day starting from the beginning, and trying each day to go a step further.

Pour some oil onto your hands,

Slowly and gently rub it on the baby's body in this sequence:

shoulders, arms, hands, chest, tummy, legs and feet.

Now you can start the massage.

Repeat each movement three times

Follow the movements shown by the arrows.

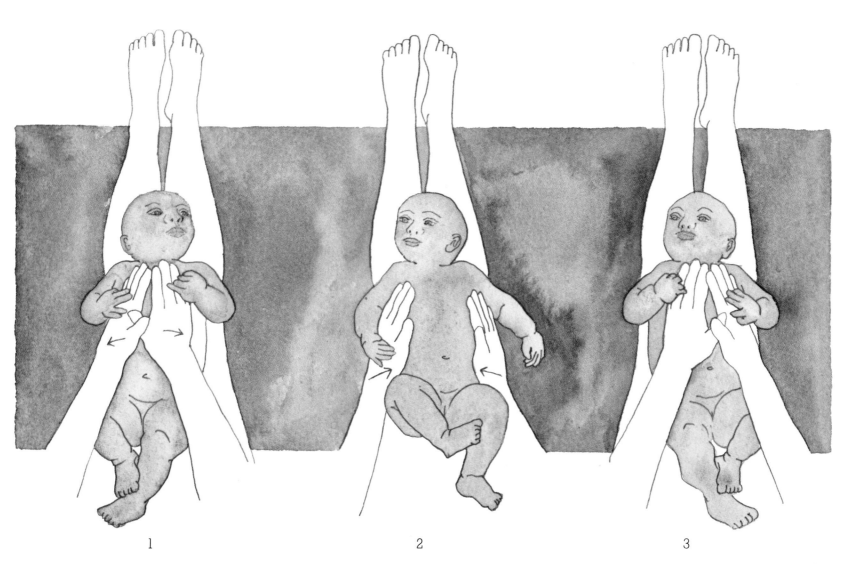

1   2   3

Follow the movements shown by the arrows.

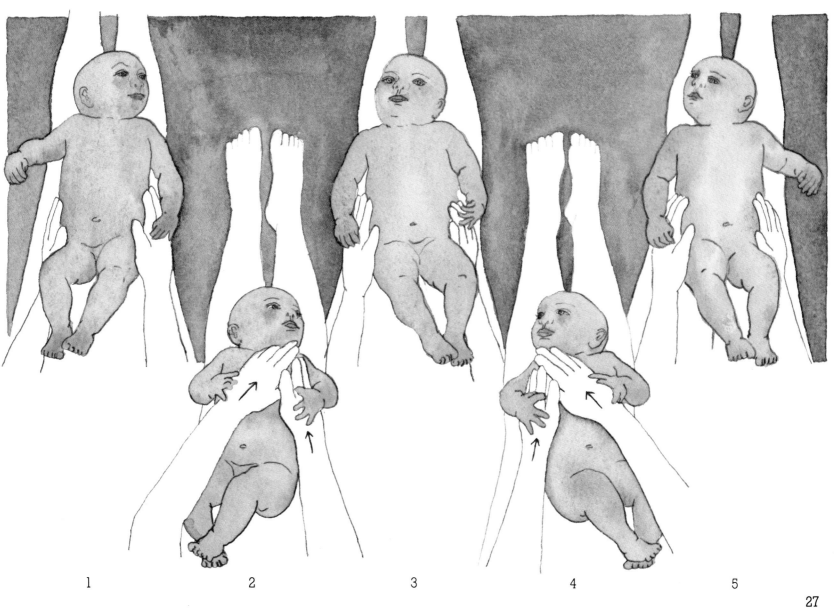

1   2   3   4   5

Arms and Hands

Always massage one arm and hand completely before starting on the other one

Arms (1)
Make a series of gentle squeezes
from the shoulder up to the hand.
Repeat this movement three times
firstly with your right hand
and then with your left.

Hands (1)
Open up baby's hand by gently
pressing with your thumb.

Arms (2)
Gently twist your hands in a corkscrew
action, beginning at the shoulder
and working up to the hand.

Hands (2)
Slide your hand slowly outwards
over baby's palm and fingers.

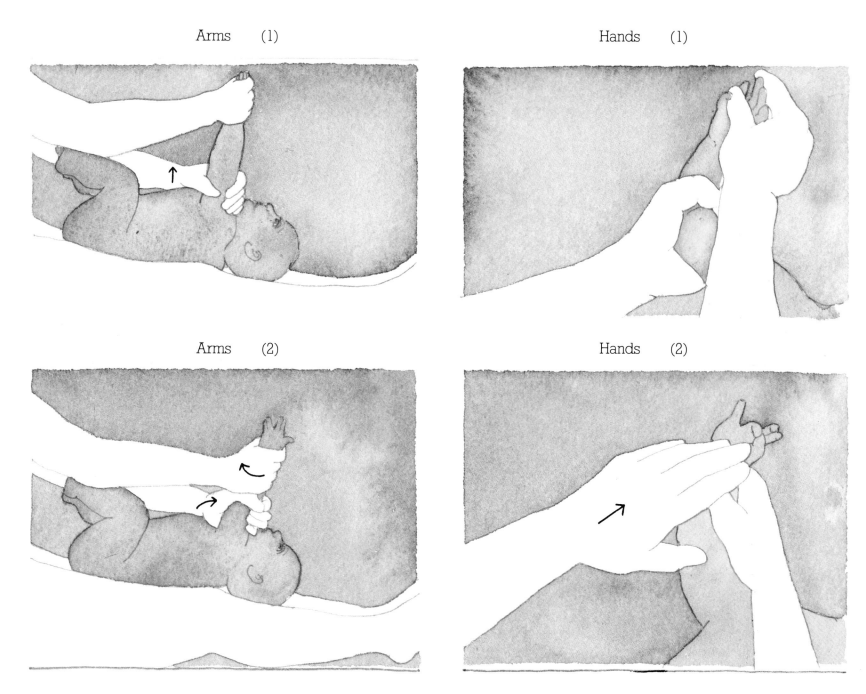

Arms (1)

Hands (1)

Arms (2)

Hands (2)

29

Tummy   (1)

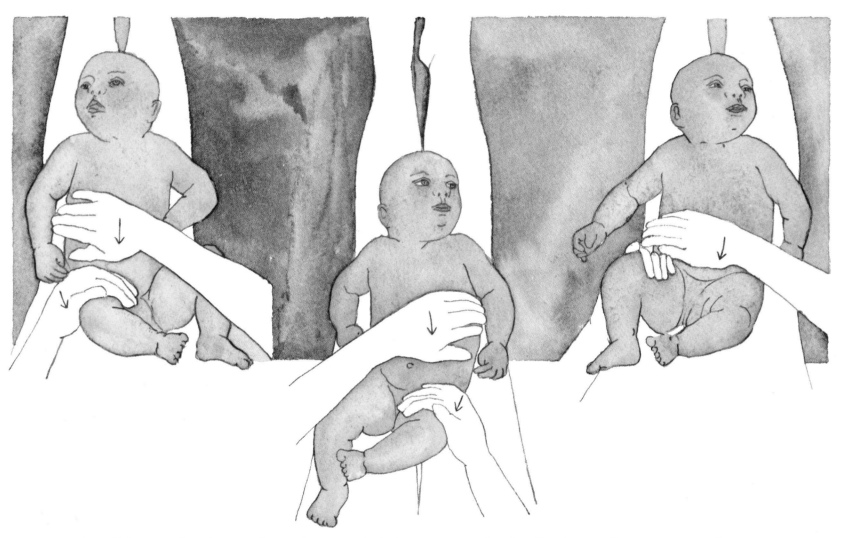

Bring your hands towards you down over baby's tummy, one after the other in a continuous movement.

Gradually work across from baby's right side to his left and back again. Repeat three times.

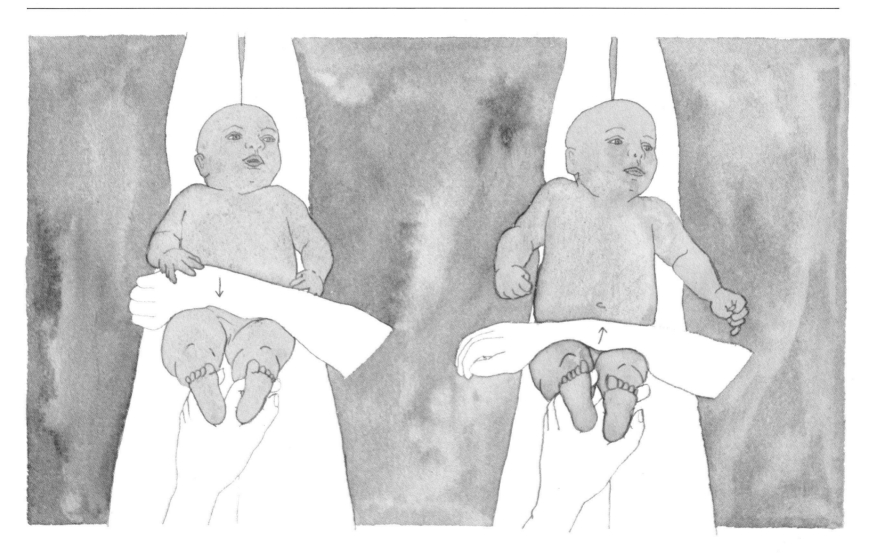

Bring baby closer to you, holding his legs vertically, and, using your forearm, massage from the
navel to the knees and back again. Do this three times and then repeat with your other arm.

Legs and Feet

Massage the legs and feet in exactly the same way
as you did the arms and hands.

Legs   (1)

Feet   (1)

Legs   (2)

Feet   (2)

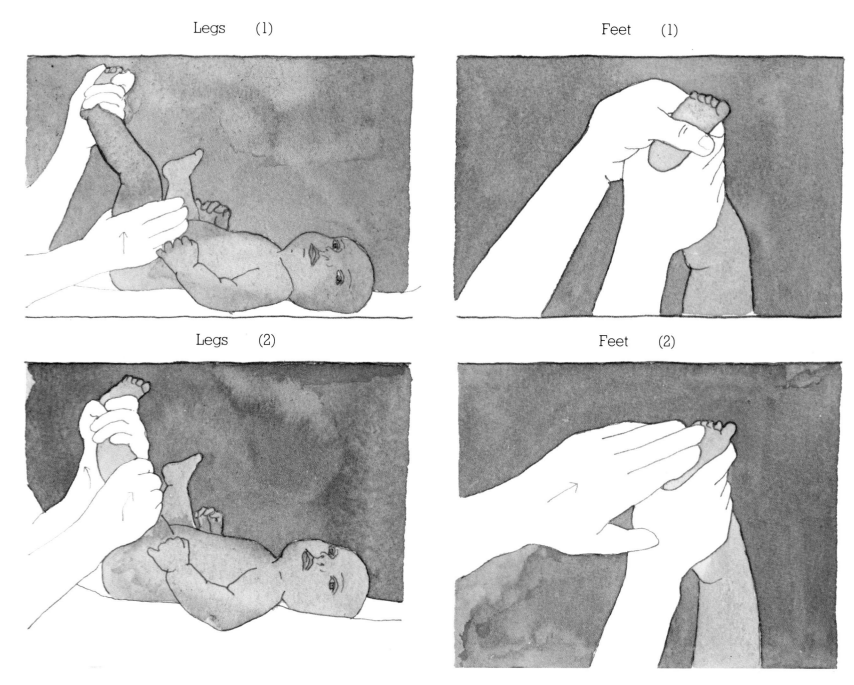

35

Back   (1)

Turn baby over and lie him across your thighs. Apply more oil.

There are three massage sequences for the back. Do each one three times.

1. Move your hands in opposite directions, working along baby's back from his bottom to his shoulders and back again.

Follow the movements shown by the arrows.

Back   (2)

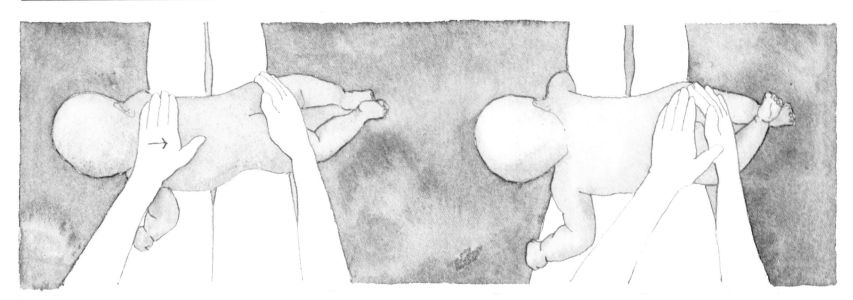

Back   (3)

39

Face

Turn baby over so that he is lying on his back

as at the start of the massage.

You do not need to apply more oil.

The facial massage should be done with a lighter touch,

taking care to avoid the eyes.

There are three sequences – do each one three times.

1A 2A 3A

1B 2B 3B

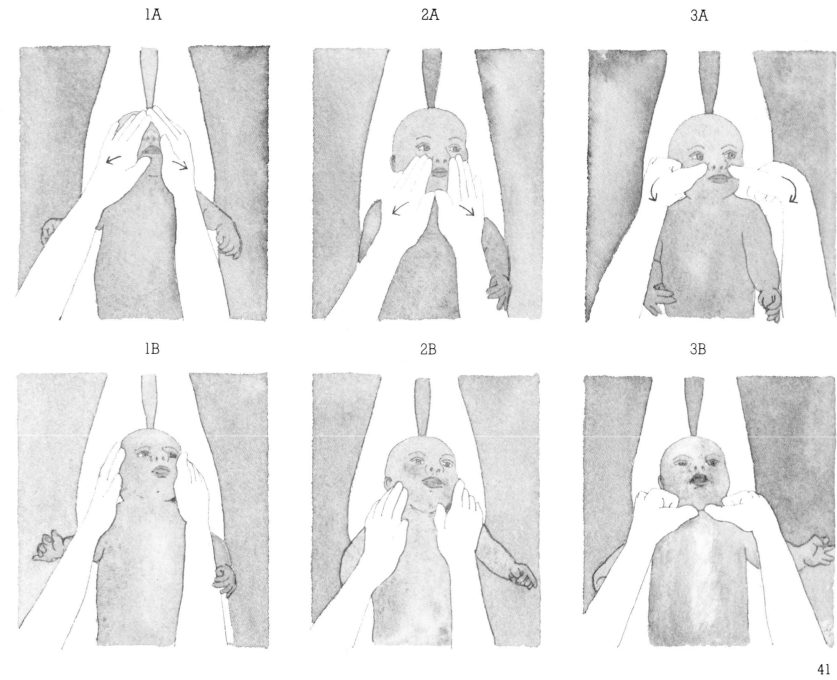

41

The exercises

After you have finished the massage, you may like to carry out
these pre-yoga-style exercises with the baby. The three exercises
are shown in the following illustrations. They will help the baby
to relax his back muscles and make them stronger.

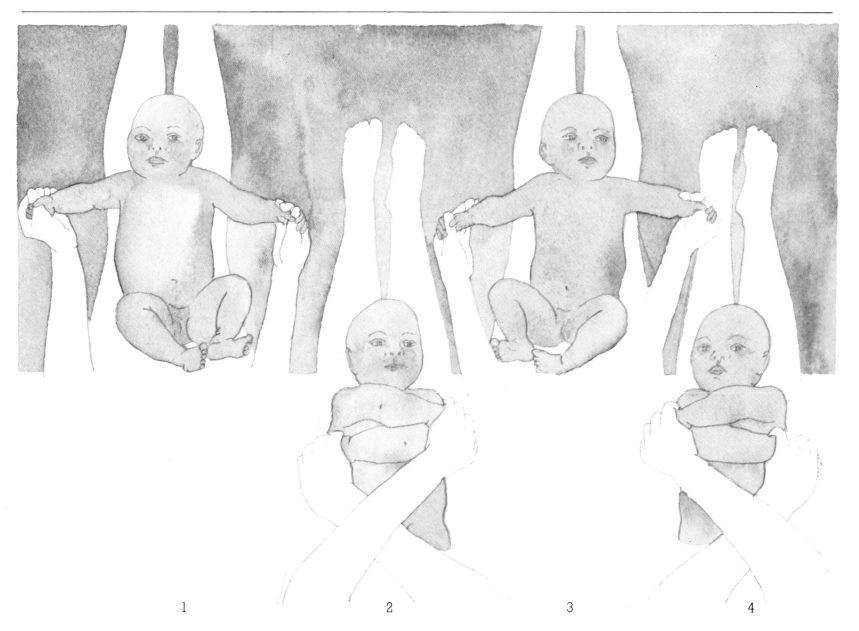

1   2   3   4

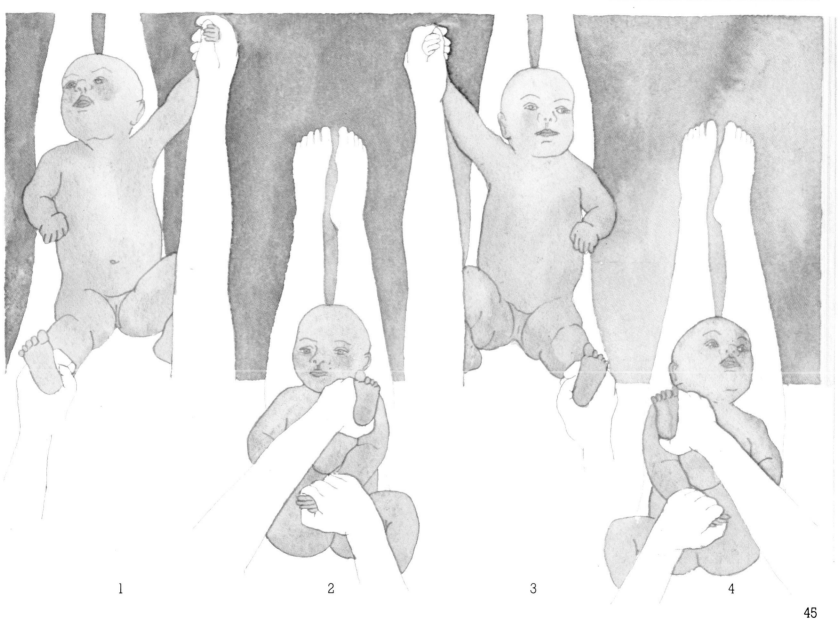

1   2   3   4

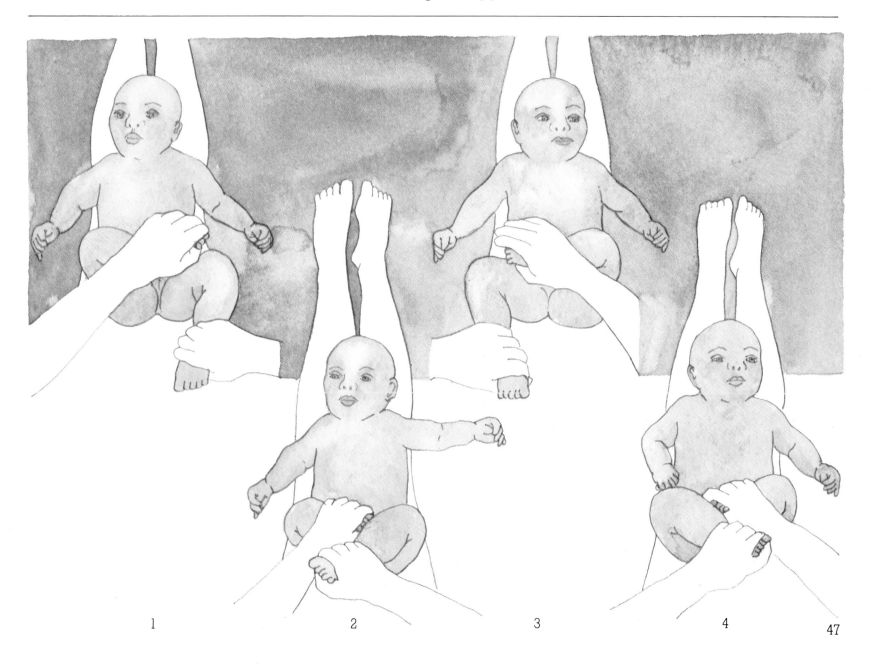

1   2   3   4   47

The bath

After you have finished the exercises, you can leave the baby on the floor, and prepare his bath. There is no need to use soap in the bath, since the oil that was not absorbed by the skin will be washed off in the warm water. Pick up the baby firmly, remembering that he might be slippery. Lower him gently into the deep water, first his bottom, and then the rest of his body. The warm water will help him to achieve an even deeper relaxation. If you have a large enough bath, and the baby is old enough, you can take him with you into your bath. This is a pleasant way for both of you to finish the massage.

After the bath, your baby will often like to have some milk, or even a full feed. The massage is an active way to relax and he will usually be hungry and thirsty. After having been massaged, bathed and fed, your baby is ready to enjoy a deep and calm sleep. What a beautiful and reassuring picture to see your baby in such a contented and relaxed sleep. I always feel that I had earned my day when I looked at my children at such moments.

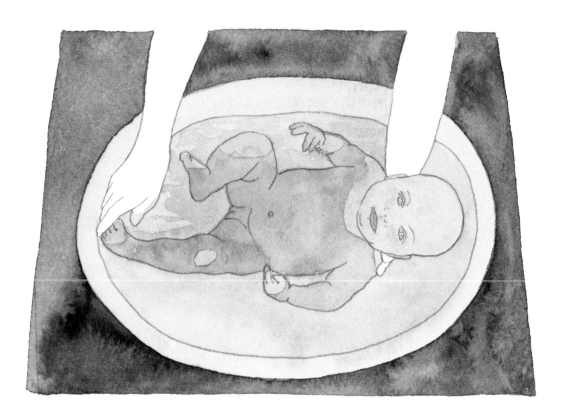

6

The Advantages of the Massage for the Baby and the Parents

The beneficial effects of the massage described in this chapter have been observed both by myself and by other parents who have learned the massage at one of my demonstrations. These advantages were observed by both fathers and mothers.

The first effect I observed after my children were massaged, bathed and fed, was the improved quality of their sleep. Very often they slept on their backs, extending fully their bodies, and with their arms outstretched. Their sleep would invariably be very deep and calm, and last for three to four hours without interruption. The picture that my sleeping children suggested was of complete satisfaction, and through their sleep they seemed able to digest and benefit from the impressions and stimulation to which they had been exposed during the active encounter of the massage session.

The massage made it easier for me to organize my new life with the baby. I usually tried to massage my children in the morning, at the same time every day, so that my day could be structured around the massage. This gave me the possibility of slowly introducing a routine for the baby's and my own activities. After the massage, I was relaxed and always able to have a couple of hours undisturbed for the household chores, and other activities. Because of that, the massage, instead of being time consuming, created time for me. It was very important to feel free without having to worry about the baby. After their sleep the children were bright and relaxed for their afternoon. In this way we both learned to adapt to each other's routine, and the massage remained a peaceful break in our day.

The ability to extend their bodies and use the space around them in a confident manner was an effect that I observed soon after the first massage sessions. Later I realized that this was the initial expression of the baby's trust of me and consequently the environment. At all times, during sleep, feeding, bathing and playing they loved to extend themselves fully, and they gave the impression to me and to others of relaxed, unafraid children. This characteristic has remained very much a part of their behaviour, and through their development they have acquired and retained a very real awareness of their own bodies. They have always been self-contained children, and they express freely their likes and dislikes. This has made it easier for me to handle my children, since I soon learned to accept them with their individual personalities.

Through the massage I learned to observe them, and to judge how far they were able to go in the different stages of their development. I became more relaxed and willing to let them explore their environment alone, bringing to it their own abilities, and trying out their skills, without any misguided parental interference or help at each minor difficulty. By being present, and yet holding myself in the background, I allowed them to pursue their own ideas, and try out new ones, in a concentrated and careful approach to the world about them.

Deep healthy sleep comes after massage and feeding.

Exploration and co-ordination.

Having learned to observe them more carefully through the massage I started to understand better the different changes that they went through in their development.

An additional benefit noticed by some mothers, especially those having difficulties in breast feeding their babies, was that the massage helped their babies to suckle better and more consistently, thus improving their feeding pattern. It was interesting to hear that suckling had improved at all feeds of the day, and not just for the feed immediately after the massage. In particular, premature babies, who in general have not yet developed fully their ability to suck, have been found to derive enormous benefit from a stroking stimulation of the face and body. Premature babies who have been systematically stroked (finger-tip massage) showed real gains in weight, and faster improvement of suckling and general development compared to premature babies who were not stroked. The need of premature babies to be touched is so great, that my friend Didi Macedo who has been applying the stroking technique (Macedo adaptation of R.I.S.S., Rice, 1977) to premature babies in several London hospitals, wrote this moving appeal to their parents:

Dearest Mum and Dad,
I am very tiny. I was born too soon and I may be too small, I know that it is rather difficult to handle me if I am in the 'glass-house' with apnoea alarm, heart-beat monitor, etc. Picking me up is even more difficult! I understand it can be no fun to cuddle me when I am not able to reward you by even opening my eyes. But I do love YOU. I cannot verbalize my feelings. However if you give me a hand I shall increase my efforts to respond to life. If you stroke my head, my face and my body twice a day you will see that I will respond to the gentle stimulation that you give me by touching me.

Mum and Dad, you can do more than watch me from outside the 'glass house' and change my nappy! I need the care of the doctors and nurses but I do need you too. I can smell you and feel your touch when you are stroking me. Do not let me have only unpleasant sensations, stroke me please, I love that!

Your baby.

Body massage provides not only a tactile stimulation of the

The sheer joy of movement.

53

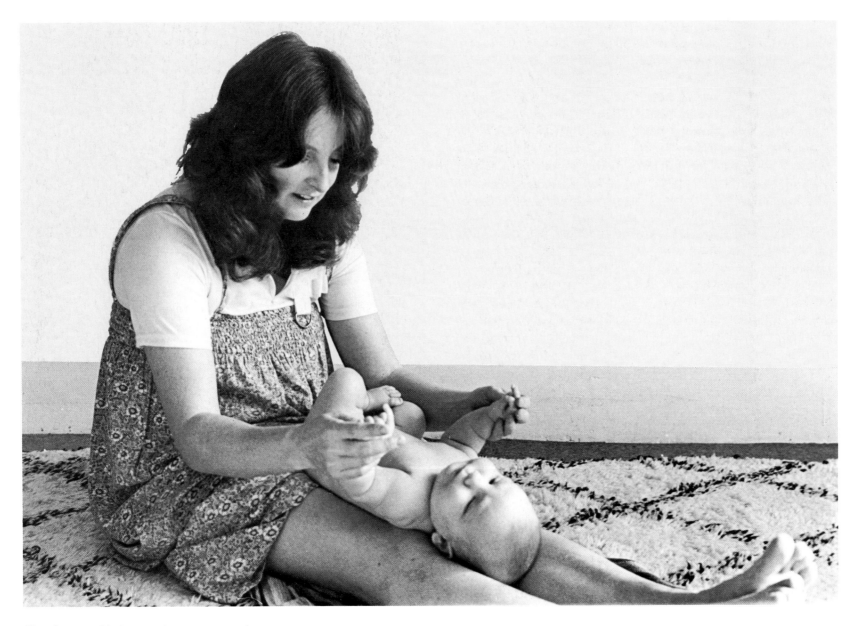

The pleasure of being together at massage time.

baby's skin, but it also reaches deeper levels of the body. It activates the blood circulation, and this is shown by the slight flushing of the skin after massage. Through the different movements of the massage, receptors in the skin, muscles and joints are activated. This dynamic process enables the baby to learn to coordinate his muscular movements. Indeed in the case of babies that for medical reasons require specific exercises, massage is often a good introduction to the exercises, allowing the baby to relax and accept more easily the exercise procedure.

Most parents have observed that the massage seems to help to relieve colic pains, especially during the first months of the baby's life. Very often the massage eases the bowel movements, and it would seem that these effects are produced both directly by massaging the baby's tummy, and also by the general relaxation achieved during the massage. The baby almost invariably urinates during massage, as a result of his state of relaxation. Initially this is a surprising experience, but one gets used to it, and accepts it as an outward expression of the deeper effects of the massage.

The position in which the massage is performed, laying the baby on the parent's legs, is especially important during the first few months of development, as it gives the baby the opportunity to feel safe, being close to the parent, and at the same time to experience freely his immediate surroundings.

A massage gives the baby the security to explore his new environment. During the massage the baby often kicks the parent, performing again, in a similar position, the movements that he made when he was inside the mother's womb. The interaction between the baby and the mother during the massage is intense, and yet allows each one to observe the other at a certain distance. The baby, lying on the bare legs of his mother, experiences the warmth of her body through direct skin to skin contact, while at the same time experiencing a separation from her. The baby can see her face, observe her expressions and feel her hands touching his body, while at the same time he is learning to become aware of his own body and to separate

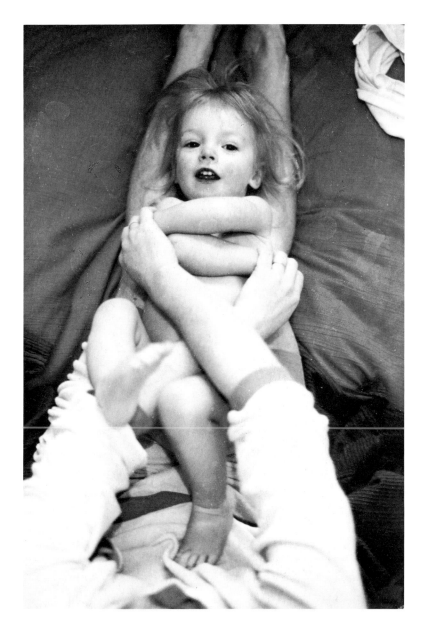

Massage is playtime; life is fun.

55

A shared bathtime completes the experience.

himself from his parent. The parent goes through the same process of getting to know her child through her hands, and this helps her to accept the child as someone in his own right, and with his own identity. By massaging her child, the parent also becomes generally more confident in handling her child. After a few sessions many parents have said that the pleasure that both they and their baby gained from the massage increased, as they became more confident with each other.

Massage is an intense interaction based on body contact, where the communication occurs almost entirely at the non-verbal level. For the infant this provides the opportunity to be understood, and to understand, through the one language – body language – that he can use in the first months of his life. After all, having fed, bathed and played with a very young baby, there is little else that one can do to communicate with him. In this respect the massage offers a very good way to be together with the baby in a deep, and yet not too serious interaction. Since we have given up the tradition of carrying our babies constantly with us, massage gives us the opportunity of renewing this intense and beneficial contact, when we are there for the baby, and the baby for us.

Profound satisfaction may be gained from touching the baby, and interpreting the body language that the baby uses in the first months of his life. This non-verbal means of communication is so important, not only for babies, that it remains one of the most intense means that human beings have of expressing their needs, desires and feelings. Thus in our verbal language, we often use the images of touch, contact and feeling to express ourselves.

7

Teaching Baby Massage to others

The experience of massaging my own children was so rewarding for me, and so enriched my relationship with my children, that it made me wish to teach the massage to other parents. Since then I have talked to many groups of people, interested for professional or personal reasons in baby massage, both in this country and abroad. I always use the film, which my husband made of a massage session, to illustrate my talk. Soon I realised that showing the film was more than a way to demonstrate the massage, it also provided an opportunity for the group to share their experiences, especially in the problems of handling young babies.

Over the past two years I have developed a method of teaching the baby massage to small groups of people. The first step consists of a short talk about the massage, accompanied by the presentation of our film. The talk is directed mainly to parents and 'expectant' parents, but has also been found informative by doctors, nurses, midwives, students, therapists and others. After a brief introduction to the baby massage, its historical aspects and its beneficial effects, followed by some practical points on how to massage a baby, I let the film speak for itself. By watching the film, it is possible to grasp the general techniques involved in the massage, and also to feel the atmosphere within which the interaction between the parent and the baby takes place. I follow the film by inviting informal discussion concerning the massage and its practice.

I have also taught the massage to small groups or individual parents accompanied by their babies. Very often 'expectant' parents were also present. This method of teaching involves demonstrating the massage step by step in a single session, during which the parent massages her own baby, under my direction. I have found it to be very important that from the start the parent attempts the massage on her own child, rather than watching me, because the most important point in the practice of massage remains, to me, the interaction between parent and baby. The basic techniques of massage are important only insofar as they allow the parent to feel confident in handling her baby and the baby to feel safe in being handled. My supervision of the massage aims only to show how the baby is held and how each step of the massage is performed and followed by the next step. I try to encourage the parent, and I hope to give her confidence to continue the massage at home, and also to help solve any difficulties that may arise.

The method of massaging that I have developed differs slightly from the traditional massage practised in India. The main point of difference is the emphasis that I give to the interaction between the parent and child, making out of each massage session an opportunity for the parent to interact with the child, while he is awake and aware, in a concentrated and yet playful mood. The whole massage is carried out with a lighter touch and is less directed towards a deep relaxation of the muscles. The baby remains awake for the whole session. Otherwise, the pattern and sequence of movements are very similar to those of the Indian massage.

My experience has shown that 'expectant' parents can also benefit tremendously from my talk and demonstration of the baby massage. From watching other parents handling their babies, and trying out the massage, they seem to come closer to the reality that will be theirs in a few months time. I think that the benefits of watching closely how to handle a baby is often underrated. In a sense, these group demonstrations give a similar opportunity for parents to learn confidence in handling their babies as was previously provided by large and extended families.

Often one demonstration is enough for a parent to learn how to massage her baby. Sometimes I organise a second demonstration, the following day, when the parents go through the sequence of the massage themselves, and we discuss any special problems that have arisen. I usually try to meet the participants of a demonstration again at a later date, to hear about their experiences of massaging their babies. I have also developed a very simple questionnaire, including questions that interest me on the outcome and effects of the massage. I try to have parents answer this, especially when I do not have the possibility of seeing them again.

I have decided to include at this stage parts of some letters that parents have sent me, so that the impressions of mothers and fathers who have used the massage may speak for themselves.

"I have massaged my son regularly at least 5 times a week. I could observe that each time he felt better and was already laughing while I prepared the oil. However, it was not always the same; sometimes he didn't like to have his chest massaged, other times his arms. But he seemed to become happier each day. I do not know if that was entirely due to the massage or simply to the discovery of his surroundings as every day he explores his environment more actively. Because we had many visitors at

Christmas I stopped the massage. At the beginning my son was still quite happy, but every night he started to sleep less well – waking up 3 to 4 times during the night instead of just once as before. He also didn't like to go to bed although he was always very tired. Two weeks ago I decided to start the massage again. Now I can really feel my hands, and I enjoy very much the massage. I am much more conscious of the pleasure of touching his body. My child also enjoys the massage more now that I also can enjoy it. He has started to sleep better again."

Another mother wrote: "I enjoyed the massage as an intense body contact with my daughter. I think she enjoyed it as well. At the beginning I started with a short form of the massage because my daughter soon became tired, and perhaps also because I was not yet very good at it. When the massage was well accepted she enjoyed it both passively and actively by kicking."
and "I massaged my child every day. While I do the massage I am able to relax so well that even my neck muscles relax. I become very concentrated and I can easily forget surroundings. My son is happy and self-contained during the massage. It seems we are able to exchange our positive energy. I am now less afraid of my son's reactions, that is I can allow him to explore and experience his environment by himself without helping him at every difficulty and without offering him the breast as a consolation. I can accept that he has his own reactions and emotions without relating them always to mine. In this way I learn to accept him in his own right with his own personality."

"Max is 5 months old now. I am not practicing the massage as conscienciously as I should, I'm afraid. In fact I massage Max whenever both of us feel like it. Sometimes we leave out days and on others we do it twice a day. The massage opened up a new way of experiencing Max's body. It's more intense and I enjoy his body more than before, that is, his skin, his muscles and muscle tone. I am happy about this new way of working and playing with Max. We have created a new and intimate atmosphere between us. Max is easy-going, relaxed and contented after the massage. He enjoys to be massaged on all of his body except his face. He smiles, laughs and giggles . . . If he has colic pains the massage does him good. he relaxes and clams down and sleeps better afterwards. Max and I have a new means of communication as well as enjoyment. We have grown closer to one another. But maybe this is a normal development. My husband is perhaps sometimes jealous of our intimate relationship, but then again he doesn't yet practise the massage and is working very hard. Thus I'm often alone with our baby."

And finally "Armin is 11 weeks old and I have been massaging him every day. Since I started with the massage I feel a close bond to my child and I like to feel and see his muscles working, his movements. I feel the need to relax and extend my own body. Armin already laughs when I start taking his clothes off, he extends his body, brings his tummy up and he is especially happy when I massage his arms and legs. After the massage he plays a lot with his own body and he is always hungry, even if he had a full feed half an hour before starting the massage. After the bath and feed he sleeps without any problem. My husband very much likes to observe us during the massage, we have both made out of it a regular ritual in our daily life. Usually I massage our son, and my husband gives him his bath afterwards. Since we started with the massage we have become less afraid of our child's colics and pains and we also do not worry any more that Armin is not moving or exercising enough."

Appendix 1

Natural oils for use in massage, their sources and properties.

Babies are traditionally massaged with one of the natural plant oils that is produced locally. Most natural oils are very well absorbed by the skin, and they have some properties that may help nourish the skin, and also stimulate other organs of the body.

Before giving a description of the different traditional oils, I think that it is necessary to include a brief note on proprietary baby oils. These oils may be used for massaging the baby, although in my experience they are not as well absorbed by the skin, so that it is often necessary to remove the residue of the oil from the skin with soap or tissues.

My choice of oil is coconut oil. It is a solid white paste at room temperature and becomes a straw-coloured liquid when warmed to 30°C. It is widely used in India, parts of rural Africa and the West Indies. It is a light oil, extremely well absorbed by the skin. It protects the skin against the sun, and helps to improve the condition of the skin in cases of skin irritation including eczema and allergies. When used regularly, it aids the skin to become smooth, and yet strong and resilient. My children never had any problems with their skin as babies, and did not suffer from nappy rash. I still use coconut oil, both on my own and on their skin.

Coconut oil can be found in any chemists' shop, or in shops selling products from India or the West Indies. It can also be produced at home from fresh coconut. The recipe that follows was given to me by a mother from India who has practised the massage with her children.

One fresh coconut is needed. When buying the coconut, make sure that it is in good condition by shaking it. If you can hear the 'water' inside it, it is fresh, if not, it is already too ripe. To open the coconut, first make a hole in one of the three 'eyes', and drain the 'water' out. You can drink this, it tastes good. Then put the whole coconut over a very low gas flame, or under a grill, and let it warm up, turning it gradually, so that its whole surface is slightly charred. Then break open the coconut with a hammer, or by throwing it on to a hard surface outside. Heating the coconut beforehand serves to free the coconut flesh from the hard shell, and it should come out without difficulty. Take the whole of the soft white flesh, and grate it into a saucepan. Add water to cover it, and bring the mixture to the boil over a gentle heat. Simmer it until the coconut milk is extracted, turning the water milky white. Then discard the coconut residue, squeezing the remaining liquid out of it in a sieve. Continue to boil the coconut milk until a layer of oil forms on the surface; it is a yellowish colour. Separate the oil from the rest of the mixture by cooling it in the refrigerator, when the oil will harden. Then keep it in a clean bottle.

Another oil that is commonly used in India is mustard oil. This oil is obtained from mustard seeds, which are widely used in Indian cookery, and as a household medicine. The oil is thought to have pain-relieving properties when it is warmed and rubbed into the skin. It seems to stimulate blood flow, and helps to clear congested lungs, and to prevent children from catching colds. The oil is strong smelling, and has a yellow colour. It is sold in Indian provision shops.

Almond oil is widely used for massage throughout the world and can be obtained at any chemists' shop. It is a heavier oil than coconut oil and it has a very pleasant scent. Like coconut oil it seems to promote the healing of skin and protects it against dryness. In India this oil is usually used for massage during the winter months.

There are a large variety of oils obtained from other plants that have been used especially in massage for adults. Often they contain some perfumed extract which may be too strong for the baby.

The best advice in using any oil for the first time is to test it on a small patch of the baby's skin, and observe if any adverse reaction, such as a rash, occurs. In such cases the oil should not be used for massaging the baby.

Appendix 2

Bibliography

Here is a selection of books I read which may be of interest to the reader.

BELL, R.Q., HARPER, L.V. – "Child effects on adults", J. Wiley & Sons, 1978.

BROOK, D., "Nature birth – preparing for natural birth in an age of technology", Penguin Books, 1976.

HERZKA, H., "Das Kind von der Geburt bis zur Schule". Bilderatlas und Texte sur Entwicklung des Kindes, 2. Auflage, Schabe, 1973 (The child from birth to school age, pictures, graphs and text on the development of the child).

KITZINGER, S., "Women as mothers", Fontana, 1977.

LEACH, P., "Babyhood", Penguin Books, 1975.

LEACH, P., "Who cares? A new deal for mothers and their children", Penguin Books, 1979.

LEBOYER, F., "Shantala – un art traditionnel – le massage des enfants", Editions du Seuil, 1976 ("Loving Hands", Collins, 1978).

LIEDLOFF, J., "The continum concept", Fontana, 1975.

MONTAGUE, A., "Touching – the human significance of the skin", 2nd. ed. Harper & Row Publ., 1978.

RICE, R.D., "Neurophysiological development in premature infants following stimulation", Develop. Psych. *13*, 69–76, 1977.

RUTTER, M., "Maternal deprivation reassessed", Penguin Modern Psychology, 2nd ed., 1981.

STERN, D., "The first relationship: infant and mother". The developing child – Ed. J. Brunner, M. Cole and B. Lloyd, Fontana, 2nd ed., 1979.

SPITZ, R.A., "Vom Dialog", Ernest Klett Verlag, 1976 (Dialogue).

LLOYD DE MAUSE, Editor, "The History of childhood – the evolution of parent-child relationships as a factor in history", Souvenir Press (Educational and Academic) Ltd., 1976.

WINNICOTT, D.W., "The child, the family and the outside world", Pelican, 1978.

YARROW, L.J., RUBENSTEIN, J.L. AND PEDERSEN, F.A., "Infant and environment – early cognitive and motivational development", J. Wiley & Sons, 1975.